I was not Born to be Broke, Broken, & Barren...

and neither were you

Brandi Ray

*"If you are willing to shift your mindset
even the slightest, you are guaranteed to change
the direction of your life tremendously."*

-Brandi Ray

I dedicate this book to my younger self — the girl raised by an extremely hardworking, single mother who understood that grind equaled survival. I watched my mother work tirelessly throughout my childhood while also showing up for us as much as she could, preparing hot meals two-three times a day, and doing it all so gracefully.

One thing I knew for sure was that it took money to survive, and as long as you kept getting up and going to the job, they would keep sending the checks. The checks might not have been enough to cover some of the luxuries in life, but they kept a roof over our heads, food in our stomachs, and nice clothes on our backs. My mother was the epitome of making broke look good.

Younger me... you saw what it was like to have just enough while feeling like it was never enough. Things were not this way because that was the only way possible, but because that was the only example that had been set for you.

Today, you write a new narrative.

Today, you uproot the deep-seated acceptance and un-tell the tale.

Today, you do it — not only for your hardworking mother but also for the chance to do the unexpected and write the story of generational wealth.

TABLE OF CONTENTS

What to expect
when expecting...
to read this book

THE BOOK SERIES, "WHAT to Expect when Expecting" was written to prepare women for the experiences that come along with carrying their unborn child.

I used *what to expect when expecting* to grab your attention so that I can share with you my expectations for every person who has the opportunity to read this book.

In the pages of "Broke, Broken, and Barren," I will share a few of my experiences from conception to completion of some very limiting mindsets and beliefs. I want you to understand the power of the mind, and how by changing one little thought or perception, you can change your entire life.

During my prayer time one Sunday morning, I kneeled in my closet a broke, broken, and barren woman, and as I prayed, in the background ministering to me was Jekalyn Carr's song, "Jehovah Jireh." The tears began to run down my face, and my silent prayers turned into wailing. Then, as I rocked back and forth, clenching both arms around my belly, I heard in my spirit these words: "Your mother didn't choose to abort you, and I need you to choose not to abort your purpose."

At that moment, I jumped up from the floor and began to run in circles around the island in my closet; I could feel purpose leaping in my womb.

Later that morning, I went to church and shared with the congregation that since I was 41 days away from my 37th birthday and that my mother had taken an enormous risk birthing me into this world due to significant medical concerns, I was declaring from that day forward that I would take every risk necessary to birth my God-given purpose into this world. So now, I invite you to witness my shift from a broke, broken, and barren young woman to a woman living in abundance, wholeness, and purpose.

My purpose is so much greater than me, and I pray that as you read this book, you will also realize the purpose that is within you. I believe if you read with expectancy, my story will change you as well.

-Brandi Ray

BROKE

Not Born to be Broke

T HE INFORMAL DEFINITION OF broke, according to Merriam-Webster, is "Not having any money." Another version calls it "penniless." Now, that is not the only definition of broke that I believe in; many people in this world are not necessarily penniless, but the pennies they do have, don't quite stretch the length of the month.

I did not grow up in a highly broke household, but we did experience life in a way that would be categorized as broke. Growing up in a small, two-bedroom, one-bathroom apartment with a single mother and two other siblings, funds were often tight; however, the broke that I experienced did not draw many sympathies because we had our needs met. Yet, there were so many circumstances where lack of money was a hindrance.

I recall watching my mother sit in her bed with mail scattered all around her, notebook and ink pen in her hand, and a furrow in her brows. She would sit there for what felt like hours, writing out each bill for the month, due dates, and how they coincided with her pay dates. This was her way of budgeting her income and expenses for the month, and many times, there would be little notes to call and let one bill collector or another know that the money might be a bit late, but it was coming.

As I grew older and became a single mother myself, I recall sitting on my own bed, bills in tow, jotting out my monthly income and expenses in the very same way. I was incredibly proud to be a reflection of my mother, who was so strong and humble, and this just felt right. Obviously, budgeting is an important task no matter your financial health. Still, the penny to paycheck habit that was birthed in me through what I had seen growing up was a habit that needed to be broken — there was no honor in having more month than I had money.

My mother had experienced this struggle based on her status as a single mother with three children, but this was not the hope that she had for us. Nevertheless, she continued to work hard and manage her coins, and I was able to witness her building financial stability, credit score, and relationship with her banking institution. My mother was an example that your current season in life does not dictate your next season in life.

When I was younger, my buckteeth were the butt of many jokes, and what people did not realize was that I had a hardworking mother who desired to get me the orthodontic care that I needed but could not yet afford it. Once I became an adult, my mother committed to bearing the expense of my braces that I had needed for so very long. Paying for my adult orthodontics was a proud moment for my sweet momma.

I also recall her inability to give my older brother his first car when he turned sixteen, but I vividly remember her excitement many years later when she could gift him a car. Her determination to contribute to our lives in this way was just a reflection of who she was, but it is disheartening when you think about those little things that money impeded. On the other hand, my little sister was pretty spoiled, but don't tell her I said so.

Being able to provide for only the bare necessities is a trick of the enemy. As long as he can lead you to think that living below your potential is the best that you can do for your life, then he holds power to keep you stuck in that place. That is what I believed to be my lifelong truth; I awakened each new day with the belief that I was simply going to have to accept the fact that I was born into a broke family and that although my husband and I were able to provide a comfortable life for our children, according to our bank statements, we still fell into the category of "broke." Rarely was there ever a time when our financial accounts were filled with an excess of our monthly expenses, and my darling, no matter how much came in, if that amount was the same as what was going out (or less than), we call that broke.

How did this cycle continue from one generation to the next? Why weren't there any strategies and plans in place to change this from being our norm? Were we satisfied with the way things were? Why were we willing to continue to work our fingers to the bone and have very little to show for it, not only at the end of our pay week but at the end of our life?

This state of being broke did not mean that we did not live happy lives because we had plenty of love and plenty of support, but we also had desires to do things that cost money, but it was money that we did not have. So, why would God give me this intense desire to help people, to give, and to do, but not provide me with the resources to do those things?

That just felt cruel. Why did I see so many people around me who had plenty of money, and they were able to go on trips on a whim and buy expensive things without it putting them in a financial bind? Why was this their story and not mine? We could ask so many questions about why our financial situation is the way it is and continue to blame those who raised us and those who raised them, or we could evaluate our life and truly get to the bottom of the lack.

I have come to a point in my life where I realize that if I truly believe what God's Word says about me and the way that I am supposed to live, then there has to be a solution to this problem that I am experiencing.

"I am come that they might have life,
and that they might have it more abundantly."
-John 10:10

So, what is abundance? Well, back to Merriam-Webster I go because I need a good understanding of what has been spoken over my life, and according to old faithful, abundance is "an ample quantity," or in simpler terms, *a relative degree of plentifulness.*

Wow! How does God's Word call me to live in abundance, which means plentifulness, and I am over here, according to the dictionary definition, living penniless?! Hold up. Time out. Foul on the play! It was at this very moment that I knew I had to call this play under review! I needed to go under those little black curtains like the referees at the Super Bowl and take a closer look at what was taking place. There had to be something that I was missing.

I was unsure about what would take place next in my life, but I knew that I would no longer accept broke to be my reality — not with the Word of God speaking as plain as day, telling me that He came that I might have ample quantity. I did not know precisely what "ample" meant, but it sounded good. You know what I did next, right? That's right ... Merriam-Webster for the win. Ample means "More than adequate in size and generously sufficient to satisfy."

At this point, you cannot tell me anything! Broke, who? I am abundant! You know why? Because I believe the Word of God more than I believe these ol' lying eyes! What I see cannot be my destiny. I believe what the Word says more than I believe that raggedy bank statement they keep sending me every month. I believe the Word of God more than I believe those up and down arrows on Credit Karma. Can I just be real with you? I even believe God more than I believe those late notices and those insufficient funds notifications from that bank down there.

Once I began to believe differently, I began to move differently. I began to pay better attention to the things surrounding my money. I began to summon my money to me. I did not see it yet in the natural, it would take a while to comprehend what had taken place within my mind, heart, and spirit, but something had definitely shifted. I realized that while I had been waiting on my bank accounts to shift, God had been waiting on my mindset to shift.

> "For as he thinks in his heart, so is he."
> -Proverbs 23:7 NKJV

In what ways has life made you feel Broke?

I want to encourage you to take a moment and become clear on which money mindsets were established in you based on your parental examples. Here are some questions that I had to ask myself as I tore down the financial barriers blocking my abundance:

- How did you see money being handled as a child?
- What were the examples set before you?
- Are those mindsets healthy? Are they permanent?

_____

_____

_____

_____

_____

_____

_____

_____

ABUNDANT

Mindset Shift:
From Broke to Abundant

Your mindset is the place where your life's experiences, your dreams, and your beliefs are stored. The things you have experienced are tallied in your mind, and the more disappointment and failure you experience, the smaller your dreams become — supporting the belief that all of the negative things happening to you are your destiny.

So, what do I mean when I say my mindset shifted? The way I saw money shifted. The way I handled my money shifted. My belief in what I was entitled to shifted. But how do we shift our mindset from broke to abundant? For starters, we have to believe the Word of God. Then, we behave according to our beliefs. Let me give you an example of how our mindsets trigger our behavior.

Think with me for a moment that I just handed you half of a lemon. I want you to visualize yourself squeezing that lemon wedge and letting the juice drip right into your mouth. If you have any experience with lemons, your jaws probably just clenched as if you were about to experience the sourest taste ever! Because of past experiences and the beliefs that you have formed around the taste and effects of lemon juice, your body responded in a way that felt appropriate.

Now, let's say I had soaked that lemon in sugar water all night and that had taken away every ounce of sourness within that lemon juice. Although that may be the case, you still expect it to be sour because of your mindset, and this expectation guided your reaction. Again, we behave according to our beliefs.

Therefore, if you believe that you have always been broke, you are currently broke, and that you will be broke for your entire life, do you think you will behave like a person with abundance? No, you are going to continue to have "broke" behavior.

Once you decide that you want to experience God's abundance, you begin to seek out things that lead to abundance. As a result, your behaviors, thoughts, and words all change, and those changes create change in your life.

> "Casting down arguments and every high thing that exalts itself against the knowledge of God, bringing every thought into captivity to the obedience of Christ."
> -2 Corinthians 10:5 NKJV

God tells us that we have the power to bring our thoughts into obedience to what His Word says, and He says that we are to have an abundant life, then why are we not bringing those thoughts of lack and poverty and being broke into alignment with His promise? We have the power; we are just not using it. Having this power is like getting your electricity turned on, buying a lamp, but not plugging it in, and wondering why you are still sitting in darkness. It is not because you do not have the power. It is because you have not taken action and connected to the source. So as you read this, I encourage you not to go another moment walking in defeat because you have not called those thoughts into alignment with God's promises for you.

Now, what is this abundance mindset that you are shifting towards? The abundance is not just speaking of financial well-being. God calls us to have abundance in peace, abundance in joy, abundance in faith, in healing, and in giving. This life that you are living does not have to remain the same. You have the power, through Christ, to shift.

I desire to live a life of abundance for so many reasons. Financially, I want to live in abundance so that I can give my family access to the fullness of this world. There are places that we will never go and experiences that we will never have if I do not tap into the abundance of Christ. Abundance opens doors of opportunity that lack can't even budge.

There is a thing called "generational wealth" that has felt like a misnomer because I have no personal experience in it. However, abundance opens those doors to generational wealth and opportunity.

I also want to experience His abundance because I have given from lack long enough. I want to be able to sow more into the areas of life that I am passionate about. I remember being a twenty-year-old single mother, working, going to college, and just not having enough to make ends meet. So many people sowed into me during that season of my life, and I have an unmeasurable desire to sow those same seeds from a place of more than enough. This is not a self-serving, self-glorified desire; this emanates from a sense of gratitude. I may never be able to show my sowers what they meant to me, specifically because some of them are no longer here on earth, but if I can return the seed into more good ground — just the thought brings me to tears.

Earlier, I mentioned the sacrifices and dedication my mother gave to us as we grew up. The thought of accessing abundance and having the ability to provide her comfort and financial peace throughout her retirement years drives me to never settle for lack.

I know with complete certainty that the abundance of God is available to you and me; thus, I have decided that I want to experience mine, and I pray that you feel that same desire. Still, for us to receive it, we must first believe it.

In what ways can you shift your mindset?

In the previous section, you identified some of your "broke" thoughts. Now, to get passionate about this mindset shift, you will need to imagine life in abundance. If you were able to live in abundance, how would that change the generations to come? Which doors will abundance open for you? Take the space below to envision a new narrative?

_____

_____

_____

_____

BROKEN

Not Born to be Broken

I REMEMBER STANDING IN THE front of a small country church we were visiting as our church choir squeezed in closely together and sang praises to God. Midway through our song, my mind flashed to a young lady as she sat on the floor holding the pieces to a broken coffee mug. She kept trying to keep the mug together, but every time she would let go, it would fall right back into broken pieces. Nearing the end of our song, I was feeling completely overwhelmed by this visual — and the most amazing part of it all was that the young lady was actually sitting right on the front row of the church (and no, she did not have an actual coffee mug in her hand).

When we finished, I knew that I had a choice to make: Would I go quietly back to my seat and allow the program to move on as planned, or would I interrupt the order of service and share the vision?

As I was known to do, I requested the microphone and walked in the obedience of God. I shared with this young lady that God was showing me her life in broken pieces and that although she had all of the pieces, she assumed that He wanted her to put the pieces back where they belonged; however, God had shown me that He was going to take her broken pieces and create a new thing. Her reaction was not one of surprise because this was just God's way of confirming for her what He had already been showing her. In my obedience in sharing this vision, she finally believed that God never created her to live in brokenness; God was ready to take her unexpected brokenness and make her not only whole, but new.

So, how was I able to identify so intimately with the young lady in the church that day? Because I had experienced brokenness. I know that I was not born to be broken, but there were circumstances in my life that had led to brokenness. This is difficult to share since I have done a pretty good job not exposing my brokenness. The first recollection of brokenness that I recall was when I was just a young girl, and I was walking out of school and headed to the bus that had so often taken me home.

I remember seeing my older brother leaning out of a bus window and calling to me that we were supposed to ride a different bus, which made zero sense to me. But I trusted him and knew that he was always looking out for me, so off I went to a new bus, with a new bus driver, and a completely different route.

But where were we headed?

My brother explained that our mom had made arrangements for us to ride this new bus and get off at a new destination, and we pulled up in front of an apartment complex that would be home for us until right before my high school graduation. This was the same day that I found out my parents were no longer going to be living together and that our family unit was changing — such a subtle break. Of course, my parents went above and beyond to make life stay as normal as living in two different homes could be; we went on family vacations together for several years following that day, and both of them made sure we still felt loved and protected and cared for . . . but there was a definite break.

As I began dating, there was brokenness that came with it. Not every man I came across was as amazing as my husband, and many of those experiences left me broken in one way or another. I had my son when I was 19, and eventually, the relationship with his father deteriorated. I remember trying to fill a void for my son because I remembered the feeling of having a broken family unit. During this season of my life, I was also trying to get through court reporting school to provide a better life for myself and my son — and let's not even talk about the trouble that broken, broken-down car of mine caused. Let's just say it was not a great experience!

I was going through life with only two hands, and while trying to work, care for my son, get through school, those hands were still holding the broken pieces together, afraid to ask anyone to help me keep it together, and afraid to let go, because I felt like I would lose it all. So, what does God's Word tell me about my brokenness?

"He heals the brokenhearted and binds up their wounds."
-Psalms 147:3 NKJV

There is a high likelihood that as you go throughout this life, that areas of your life will experience brokenness. I have watched as people close to me have buried parents and children and things that seem wholly unbearable. People have experienced illnesses and loss in a way that seems unrecoverable. Brokenness may occur, but we have God's promise that He will heal our brokenness and bind up those shattered places.

I want to encourage you today that if you are in a season of brokenness, that is not your final destination. But, you can be made whole. Just like the woman with the issue of blood, as she told the whole truth about her infirmities, her faith made her whole. I believe that God is waiting on our faith to meet his power so that we can experience wholeness.

You were not born broken, and you were not born *to be broken.* Life may have happened, and you may find yourself in a state of brokenness, but you do not have to remain there. You can choose to be whole.

In what ways has life broken you?

Being honest about brokenness is often challenging. Not only do you have to identify the brokenness, but you also have to identify the root. This is not an attempt to place blame on the source of your hurt but to free you from that broken place. Identify the brokenness and the source so that healing can begin?

_____

_____

_____

_____

_____

_____

_____

WHOLE

Mindset Shift:
Broken to Whole

I N ORDER TO SHIFT our minds from broken to whole, we have to decide that we are not the sum of the things that have happened to us, but we are who God says we are:

> For you formed my inward parts; you covered me in my mother's womb. I will praise you, for I am fearfully and wonderfully made; marvelous are your works, and that my soul knows very well.

> My frame was not hidden from you when I was made in secret, and skillfully wrought in the lowest parts of the earth. Your eyes saw substance, being yet unformed. And in your book they are all written. The

days were fashioned for me, when as yet there were none of them.

How precious also are Your thoughts to me, O God! How great is the sum of them! If I should count them, they would be more in number than the sand; when I awake, I am still with you."

-Psalms 139:13-18 NKJV

What does this amazing Scripture mean to me, and what does it have to do with wholeness? First, it tells us that God formed our inward parts; He knew the heart and compassion that we would have that would open us to being broken by people and situations. Then, it says that He covered us in our mother's womb, which tells us that even before we were born, we were at risk of harm, and that is when He first began to cover us.

Now, this just dropped in my spirit; just because you might be experiencing brokenness, that doesn't make you breakable. That may sound confusing, but I want to let you know that although some things may make you feel a sense of brokenness, irreparable things are to be tossed out — there is no experience that God cannot repair. No amount of damage can be done to make you useless to God.

The Scripture goes on to say that "I will praise you for I am fearfully and wonderfully made," so you were made with great reverence and uniqueness. "Marvelous are His works" is a representation of the amazement that we feel when we experience His grand purpose for our lives.

Oftentimes, we feel that we are flawed in one way or another, but do we honestly believe that our creator made a mistake in forming us? When we were created, God saw to each intricate detail, and nothing was hidden from Him. We are unique perfection. Therefore, when it says, "Your eyes saw substance yet unformed and in your book they are all written…" Wow! Before we even had anything within us and before we impacted this world in any way, God already saw the value that we would add. He saw the substance of our character and the goodness of our hearts. Before we began to do good, He had it written in "The Book." I can barely take this Scripture line by line because my heart feels overwhelming gratitude for the care shown to me at creation. God has truly been so good, despite the situations that felt like brokenness.

The next line says, "The days were fashioned for me when there were yet none." Like seriously! Before the days even began, God fashioned them just for me. As an analogy, I think about an expectant mother who can not help herself as she sees the clothing that she already knows would be perfect for her baby girl; she has beautiful things awaiting her before her first day on earth.

Daughter, sister, friend, that is the same way our heavenly father was before our days even began! He fashioned our days with goodness, and grace, and joy, and wholeness! When I think of them, they are numbered like grains of sand! When I think of the goodness of The Lord and try to count the ways He's blessed me, it is equivalent to going to the beach and attempting to count grains of sand! There is no way to count all of the ways He has blessed us.

"And when I wake, I am still with you." I do not believe this refers to a physical slumber, but when I rise from my brokenness, I am still with you. You are still with me. No matter where life has taken you and what you have experienced, I comfort you with these words, "He is still with you."

Let your conduct be without covetousness; be content with such things as you have. For He Himself has said, "I will never leave you nor forsake you."
-Hebrews 13:5

Although I experienced brokenness in various forms, I believed that God wanted me to be made whole and that He could make me whole again. Just like the young lady in my vision, I had to give every broken piece over to God and trust Him to know what to do with it.

Once I relinquished my hold on the pieces, my hands were free to do more, and there was so much peace in not trying to heal myself. I did not necessarily see the healing and transformation overnight, but I looked up one day, and my life was unrecognizable. My childhood brokenness was healed in the sense that I continued to be strengthened in my relationship with my parents even through the divorce.

I don't even know how The Lord snuck my husband in on me. I was head-down, mommy-ing it up, and excelling in school, when out of nowhere, it seemed, there was this handsome, confident young man who walked in and loved me unconditionally, and more importantly, loved my son as if he were his flesh and blood.

If I'm honest, we get comfortable in our brokenness to the extent that wholeness is uncomfortable at first glance. I recall the fear and uncertainty as things began to just work in my favor. There were people who did not understand his interest in me as a single mother, but he never wavered. At the young age of 21, we started dating, and by the time we turned 24, we were getting married and buying our first home. My son experienced family in the way that I had before my parents divorced; we vacationed and valued our time together as a family.

After a year of marriage, we welcomed our beautiful daughter into the world, and we are right now approaching thirteen years of marriage. The Lord had taken every broken piece of my life and made something so beautiful with it.

I know that is a beautiful picture that I just painted, and even though each day is truly a blessing, I dare not lead you to envision perfection because we are far from that. The hope is that as I share bits and pieces of my story, you will see what is possible when you allow God to lead. Every day won't be without problems, but there will always be a positive solution.

And, if you find yourself in the midst of your brokenness right now, I pray that you begin to seek wholeness, understanding that God is willing and able to make you whole. He can heal the wounds you have carried since childhood and restore the pieces you may have lost along the way.

If you are a young lady dealing with brokenness from relationships, I encourage you to fix your focus on Christ and your future, the man that He has just for you will find you when your head is down, and your focus is fixed. Be where you were called to be, doing what you were called to be doing, so that your husband's directions will lead him straight to you!

However, before you experience wholeness in your being, you need to experience wholeness in your mind. Choose today to take your mind off of the brokenness. Choose today to take your mind off of the people and things that have caused you brokenness. Take your hands off of the broken pieces and allow God to take over. You may be broken right now, but you can choose today to begin your journey to wholeness.

In What Ways can you shift your mindset?

For some of us, brokenness formed at such a young age that we do not even know what being whole feels like. What has happened to you, but it is not who you are? How can you begin to change your thoughts so that they align with God's promise of wholeness?

_____

_____

_____

_____

_____

_____

_____

_____

BARREN

Not Born to be Barren

THE WORD "BARREN" IS often used to refer to a woman who cannot have a child. I have always just taken that to be the definition, and it's often mentioned when speaking of Hannah in the Bible, who was without a child until she cried out to The Lord and He granted her request to bear a child.

As I began to write this chapter, I decided that I wouldn't just assume that to be the definition, and I went to my favorite resource and looked up the meaning, and the first thing to come up was not the words "unable to reproduce." Instead, it said, "Not reproducing." The fact that not reproducing was the very first definition jumped off the pages at me, because let's be clear, just because you are not doing something, that does not mean that you are necessarily incapable of doing said thing.

So, for those who know the story of Hannah, she suffered through painful and shame-filled years in her family as she went without bearing a child, and even worse, her husband had children with another woman. At some point in her life, Hannah had been labeled barren, and she experienced many years of barrenness. Still, as I previously mentioned, one particular day, she decided that she no longer wanted to experience barrenness, so Hannah cried out to The Lord and asked Him to grant her desire to have a son. The story details how Hannah bore a son and went on to live a blessed life. Nothing changed with Hannah physically, but her belief in what was possible with the Lord's help took her from "not producing" to "with child."

Like in Hannah's story, some of us have been labeled "unable to do or be something" in life, and due to that label, we have gone through life not producing — which brings up personal feelings for me because, at the time of my mother's pregnancy with me, she had suffered complications in a prior pregnancy. Her doctor had advised her to abort me, as there was a fear that I would not make it to term, and the complications threatened my mother's life. I can only imagine the worry and the fear my mother felt as she carried what could have possibly been fatal in her womb. I have an older brother, so she was already a mother, which brings even more responsibility. My mother talked with her doctor, and they scheduled the termination of the pregnancy, but as you read this, you already know that it did not happen.

We often assume our barrenness only refers to bearing physical children; however, it is about so much more than childbirth — there are some gifts and businesses and ministries that have been stifled due to our feeling barren. I do not know about you, but I know I was not born to be barren. If God did not have a great purpose and a great plan for my life, then I would have been aborted back in the summer of 1983, and I would not be challenging you to live out your life's purpose right now!

I praise my momma so highly for her bravery in the face of the lies of the enemy! I'm sure that doctor meant no harm, but that was the devil's attempt to keep me from entering this world and challenging the spirit of doubt and fear and lack and complacency that is hindering your reproduction system!

I have two beautiful children, a boy and a girl, and I have been told many times that I was called to have more children because the Bible tells us, "And you, be ye fruitful and multiply, bring forth abundantly in the earth, and multiply therein" (Genesis 9:7). Nevertheless, I know God has shown me that the gifts He placed within me were created to bring forth abundance and to multiply it in the earth.

In my prayer time this morning, before I sat down at my computer, I prayed over those who would read the words that I write. I asked God to take away the barrenness that hinders us from multiplying our gifts in the earth. I began to think of when I carried my children in my womb. I recall making many decisions to make sure that they were well-nurtured even in my belly. The moment I found out that I was carrying each child, I began to nurture them. Being pregnant, there were places I could no longer go and things I could no longer do; it became my responsibility to ensure their development.

I recall that once my children were born into this world, I ensured that they were covered and protected, and I was intentional about watching them grow. I think about how passionate I am about seeing my babies reach their fullest potential in this world because I know if they fully develop and mature, that they have the power to impact a nation.

I am here to share with you that God has placed some greatness in your belly in the form of purpose. You have a very specific purpose, and just because you may not currently be producing, that does not determine what you are capable of.

I want you to look the doctor of lies, the enemy, right in the face and tell him that you will not abort the promise that God has for your life. You are carrying a unique gift that is needed in this world, and it is your responsibility at this moment to begin to nurture it.

Just call me "Clear Blue," because Ma'am, Sir, you are pregnant! You are expecting. You are not barren. It is time for us to start living with "Genesis 9 and 7" intentionality and reproduce abundance.

If you've ever thought you were pregnant, were hoping to find out you were pregnant, only to later be disappointed and decide that you were wrong, I'm sure that's how you've felt about this calling on your life. There have been moments where God has given you a glimpse of the promise, and you were hopeful. Then, as time went by, you decided that you must have been wrong, so you decided that you weren't carrying anything and accepted the label of being barren of purpose.

Right now, I declare and decree that I was not born to be barren . . . and neither were you.

In what way has life made you feel barren?

I want to be honest about the agony of feeling empty and help you to get clear on the "what" and the "why" so that you can move on to focus on the "how." Take a moment to reflect on the following questions: In what areas of your life have you felt barren? What made you feel barren? Who made you feel barren? What are some things you desired to produce into this world, but you aborted? How will we shift in this season?

_____

_____

_____

_____

_____

_____

_____

_____

_____

_____

_____

_____

_____

_____

_____

_____

_____

_____

_____

_____

_____

_____

_____

_____

PURPOSE

Mindset Shift:
I am Carrying Purpose

NOW THAT YOU HAVE accepted that the doctors were wrong, and you are able to reproduce, are you ready to give up those things that threaten the delivery of your purpose? When it comes to being pregnant physically, we know that many give up cigarettes, alcohol, parties, travel, et cetera. So, I challenge you today and ask you, what are you going to have to give up in order to bring your purpose to term?

When I think of my purpose and the way God has gifted me with pulling purpose from others, I know that some things that I have to give up in order to see this ministry, this business, this impact come to maturity are things like fear, self-doubt, defeat, self-pity, laziness, distractions — and the list goes on. I realize that none of these things serve in nurturing my calling; if I don't overcome the fear that others won't receive me, or that I can't help others, or if I continue to feel sorry for myself because others aren't recognizing my gift or giving me a seat at their table of success, or if I'm not willing to sometimes go to bed late and get up early with this baby, I can guarantee, that I will never see the power of what God created within me.

I am challenged that Mom had the bravery to birth me into this world AMA (Against Medical Advice), so I have decided that I have to have that same bravery when walking in my life's purpose. My mother did not take on that medical risk for me to come into this world and live barren.

Now that I've shared with you my "why," I want you to get clear on your why. Why will you show up for your purpose on the days that you don't feel like it? Why will you show up for your purpose on the days where it feels at-risk? Why will you show up and nurture and develop and mature your purpose, although someone has told you that you were barren? Once you know your "why," I encourage you to channel your inner momma-bear. That's the nickname my husband has for me, simply because he has witnessed the intensity that arises in me when I sense a threat to my children, whether it be physically, emotionally, or mentally. If you ever want to see a momma act a fool, mess with her babies.

Your purpose is your baby. Your purpose is what you bear in your womb, and you nurture, and birth, and develop, and raise. Lord, we did not even talk about the sacrifices that are necessary when raising our babies! How many times did you have to put them before yourself? Put their needs before your own? Spend money.... should I go there?

Your purpose has the potential to make a major impact in this world, and you can stand back like a proud momma when you watch the difference it is making.

- Are you ready and willing to go from Barren to Purposed?
- Are you willing to give up the things that don't nurture the gift that is developing in your womb?
- Are you ready to protect the gift and sacrifice for it?

When God gives you this gift and purpose, you have to be willing to sow into it. It is going to consume your time, your emotions, and your money. But if you do it just right, in your older age, the tables will turn, and your investment into your baby will reap a reward for you!

I am well aware that someone may be reading this book and feeling left out because you may not have biological children to appreciate the comparison fully. But even if you don't have children, you were once someone's child. You can recall the sacrifices your parents made for you. Even if it was a grandparent or a family member, whoever nurtured you, sacrificed for you, helped you become who you are today, it requires that same kind of care. And if no one showed up for you, think about how much you wish that they had and how desperately you wanted someone to be willing to fight for your future. Your purpose feels the same way.

Regardless of how it looked for you, you get to choose how it looks for your purpose. It is a gift that God has given you. It serves a purpose to this world, and it is your responsibility to see it through.

In what ways can you shift your mindset?

Be brave. Be honest. Be hopeful. What is your purpose? How can your purpose change your life? How can your purpose change those around you? How pleased would God be with seeing your purpose fulfilled? Are you ready to live on PURPOSE?

_____

_____

_____

_____

MY MINDSET SHIFT

My Mindset Shift

As I shared with you about my mother being instructed to abort me, I did not mention that because of the condition, the only way they felt the pregnancy had any potential to be viable was for her to attend bi-weekly appointments in Houston, Texas, which is about four and a half hours south of our little one-red-light town (there were no red lights back in '84 when I was born).

My mother and father were left in what felt like an impossible position, yet my mother informed Dr. Green that she wanted to do everything possible to survive this pregnancy. Eventually, arrangements were made for the specialist to fly to Dallas (about an hour drive) twice a month to care for my mother and the unborn child (turned amazing, powerful woman of God).

As my mother went week by week, month by month, trimester by trimester, she was told that it appeared that I was going to need a full blood transfusion immediately upon delivery, which they had to sign off on and approve beforehand. Despite the thought of this delivery and all of the lingering complications, my mother soldiered on.

Then, May 8, 1984, rolled around, and it was time. To everyone's surprise, I came into this world completely healthy, with no need for a blood transfusion (I was covered in the blood of Jesus!), and my mother had a safe delivery!

Reflecting on my journey into this world, I could only stand in awe at how hard God fought for me to be here living out my life's purpose, and because of that, I am also determined to fight for you and your purpose! My mother was brave and bold and determined to deliver me into this world AMA against medical advice, and I am committed to helping you birth your purpose into this world AMA (against mediocre advice)!

Dreamers and purpose pursuers are often discouraged on their journey due to the opinions of mediocre minds. It is challenging for others to see the greatness in you when they have yet to see their greatness.

Because of the opinions of others, many people never go after their goals, never chase their dreams, and dare not get in a purpose pursuit.

I am here today to ask you to sign an AMA. I need you to decide that you are willing to risk it all to birth your purpose into this world. And don't get it twisted, frequently that mediocre mind is sitting right between our own ears. I'm sure you were high-fiving me when I was referring to outside mediocrity, but it is the mediocrity that we carry around with us daily that causes the biggest delays.

Many of us have accomplished a minuscule level of success, and we have gotten comfortable right in that place. In our communities, graduating high school is the highest level of achievement most of us expect, and Lord help us if someone goes on to obtain an Associate's degree. Now, don't take that as an insult because I didn't even do the latter. I did, however, receive a certificate from the State of Texas that licensed me as a certified court reporter, and because of that, I was able to sustain a reasonably nice salary for myself. But there was still so much purpose left unfulfilled in my life.

It was at the beginning of 2021, as I sat with my amazing husband — who loves me more than I could have ever imagined — my handsome and compassionate teenage son and my brilliant and ambitious daughter in our brand-new home that we had built from the ground up. At that moment, it felt like everything should feel right in my world, but there was this unsettling that I could not shake. When I first started to feel this, I thought there was something wrong with me, but as I went on a 21-day fast, it became apparent that purpose was calling from deep within me. I returned to the thing that I was passionate about, that thing that only I could do, as myself, which was to write, speak, and assist others in pursuing their purpose. The minute I acknowledged that purpose was calling, I answered the call and never looked back. Coming off the tail-end of a year like 2020, I felt a strong sense of urgency to just empty myself of every gift and talent and every ounce of purpose.

This mindset shift was one of astronomical value, and the shifting gave me a strong sense of joy and fulfillment. I decided to pursue my purpose full-out, no longer hiding behind the veil of mediocre thinking. I was no longer going to tell myself that I should just be thankful for my current success — which had led to some earthly gain — when God was waging war while I was in my mother's womb, for me to fulfill His purpose for my life while I am here on earth.

Your fight for purpose may not have started in the womb, but I am confident that throughout your life, you have been at war with something standing in the way of you living in the fullness of your purpose. I want you to ask yourself, is the life that you are living fulfilling your life's purpose? Does it feel like you are doing all the things with all of the gifts and talents and desires God placed inside you? One thing about purpose, it always serves, so is your life serving others?

If your answers to those questions were not a resounding "yes," then I encourage you to identify the problems in your mindset that are holding you back. Then, shift some things around that will set your purpose free!

Sign here if you are pursuing Purpose A.M.A.

_____

In what ways can you get clear on what mindset shifts you need to make?

_____

_____

_____

_____

_____

_____

_____

_____

PURPOSE
PURSUER
PRENEUR

Are you a Purpose Pursuer Preneur?

THESE THREE WORDS CAME to form my very first business as an entrepreneur. The journey was very intimidating as I embarked on my mission to make the thing that I was most passionate about profitable for me so that one day I can genuinely live this dream life as a full-time servant and business owner.

My definition of a purpose pursuer preneur is *a woman of faith, fearlessly pursuing her purpose in a profitable way.* Yeah, just say, "Man!" if that's you, like we do when reading the Bible.

So, I am a woman of faith, pursuing my life's purpose, and doing it in a way where I can provide income to my family. But what I quickly discovered is that when you are in the will of God, you do not just gain income . . . you access abundance! And, as we have already discussed, to live in abundance is to live with more than enough, as the abundance that God promises us is far more than monetary value.

> "The thief cometh not, but for to steal, and to kill, and to destroy: I am come that they might have life, and that they might have it more abundantly."
> -John 10:10

"Steal" might be in reference to money, but to kill and destroy refers to all of the other areas of our life that are under attack. The Lord comes that we might have life, which combats the kill theory, but the more abundantly covers the steal and destroy aspect. Our money is at risk of being stolen by the enemy. When we do not live out God's purpose for us, we have essentially allowed the enemy to steal our fullness and plentifulness. To destroy refers to our peace, our joy, our well-being. And The Lord comes that we may have more than enough joy, more than enough peace, and exceeding well-being.

Therefore, you have to ask yourself, if He has come that I might have this abundant life, will I choose to pursue this purpose-filled, abundant life and make His coming worthwhile? So, to help you to live the life of a purpose pursuer preneur, I first need you to identify your purpose.

Then, once you have your purpose identified, I need you to pursue it. Now, the most common pursuit that most of us are aware of is a police pursuit. Many of us have been traveling through town when suddenly, we witness a full-on police chase — where a suspect is fleeing, and an officer is in full pursuit. This pursuit may look untethered and out of control, but in all actuality, the officer has been given tactical training and sophisticated strategies to assist in the apprehension.

In the same way, when you are in pursuit of your purpose, you are going to need some tactics and strategies that will assist you when debris comes up in your way and obstacles arise because if you are pursuing your purpose with no strategy in place, you will most likely have to call off the pursuit.

My heart's desire is that you apprehend your purpose and then make it profitable to release financial abundance for your life.

What is your purpose, how will you pursue it, and how can you make it profitable?

_____

_____

PURPOSE
MID-WIFE

Purpose Mid-wife: Push!

A MIDWIFE IS A HEALTH professional trained to support and care for women throughout their pregnancy, during labor, and after birth. One of the primary purposes of a midwife is to assist you in delivering with little to no intervention. The midwife also provides services for a brief period following the birth.

Some of the qualities of a great midwife are a caring and understanding attitude, providing emotional and mental strength, having good observation techniques, patience, maturity, taking on great responsibility in your care, and having the ability to act on their own initiative. It is time for you to birth the purpose you are carrying, and I am here to be your midwife.

As a purpose midwife, I care so deeply about helping you birth the purpose that God has placed in your womb. I understand that it would be much easier to carry the purpose indefinitely than to go through the pains of labor, but the gift that is waiting on the other side is so worth it. Therefore, I am here to walk with you through the emotional and mental limits that have complicated your birthing process. Through my personal experiences, I have the patience and maturity necessary to induce your labor. It is my responsibility to create an environment conducive to a safe and exciting delivery of your purpose.

My desire as a purpose midwife is to proudly look back at all of the precious gifts I have had a hand in birthing into this world. Your purpose and your gift are needed here, and I want to help you deliver them. I will be there to guide you, to hold your hand when you need to squeeze, and I will help usher your purpose into this world, but none of that will be possible unless you are willing to push.

There have been times where women have had to give birth all alone. Women have gone into labor with no one around, and they have birthed their own babies; however, this is not a safe practice — it is scary, and it is ill-advised if that is ever suggested to you. The same can be said about your purpose. Many people have gone through the process of birthing their purpose alone, and that leaves room for many complications. If you are doing this alone, there is no one to assist you with things that are out of your reach, there is no one to calm you when fears and doubt arise, and there is no one to catch the vision and help you to birth it.

In the birthing room, there are many risk factors, and as you birth your purpose, there will be risk factors such as the limits that have been placed on your beliefs, the negative influences that you have partaken in, and things such as imposter syndrome and analysis paralysis. As your midwife, I will help you to remove the limits that have been deep-rooted in you through what you've experienced and what you've seen from others. Many of us cannot see the beauty in our own purpose because we have seen the limited successes of others around us. We begin to believe that because such-and-such never fully reached their potential, then that level of purpose fulfillment must be out of reach. You need a midwife in your ear, reminding you that those are false limits, and if you give it one big hard push, your purpose will begin to come forward.

You may be a person who has been told that you will never amount to anything, or because your momma was not this, or your daddy was that, then you will only be this. You may have had a teacher tell you what they felt you were incapable of achieving, or your own voice may be chanting some very defeating self-talk, but I will drown out those sounds as I repeat, you are capable, you are filled with purpose, you have the potential to do great things. The more you hear empowerment, the less power those negative influences will have on you and your purpose.

Imposter syndrome, some people say, does not exist; however, as a person who has felt like an imposter on the stage of life, I am here to tell you that, whether it is clinical or symbolic, this syndrome is impactful and has the potential to stop you in your tracks.

Some of the symptoms of imposter syndrome are feeling like a fraud, self-doubt, fear, and even worthlessness. Many people cope with imposter syndrome by stepping back from their purpose, coming to a standstill, or hoping to go unnoticed. This syndrome makes you feel like you've done something wrong by believing in yourself and your greater purpose. Some of the causes of imposter syndrome are promotion, recognition, success, and literally, pursuing your purpose. The moment you decide to pursue your purpose, you have exposed yourself to the disease of imposter-itis, and the symptoms will eventually be onset.

So, how do we cure or treat imposter syndrome? One of the first cures that I discovered when self-diagnosing and home-remedying my experience was to go to my creator. I asked God, "Am I being an imposter, or is this who you called me to be?" Once I felt confirmed in my spirit that I was authentically walking in my purpose, I knew that the treatment protocol would be to keep pushing, keep going, keep pursuing. The further I walked into my purpose, the more I felt validated in being there. The more I took myself out of the equation and focused on the people my purpose was called to serve, the less I felt the symptoms, and the moment I experienced someone walking into their purpose through me living out my purpose, I felt cured! It was then that I knew I was not carrying out any fraudulent behavior and that I was who God said I was. There were no imposters in the room.

So, whether you want to call it imposter syndrome or just plain old self-doubt, I encourage you to get to the root of the symptoms, come up with a treatment plan, and overcome that lying and limiting belief. People are waiting on you to stop doing what you think you were purposed to do and to start being who you were purposed to be!

Now, when you convince yourself that you are not an imposter, you begin to get excited about your journey to purpose. In this online society that we live in, there is so much information and so many tools right at our fingertips, so we usually strike out down this path of gathering. We hop on Youtube and binge-watch videos that are connected to our purpose. We get on Google, and we look for resources that will sharpen our skills and techniques. We pop onto the litany of social media platforms and watch the reels and stories and lives of influencers who seem to be making the impact in the world that we seek for ourselves.

All of these things can be very helpful in keeping you motivated to pursue your purpose because often, you are not surrounded by like-minded people who are also pursuing their purpose, so those connections and insights can keep the fire lit beneath you. So how can this become a problem for you?

Let's talk about analysis paralysis. We all know the meaning of paralysis, "The loss of the ability to move," so how does that come into play when speaking of analysis? Well, many people on their purpose journey and pursuit begin taking in all of this valuable information, and it becomes overwhelming to them. There is such a thing as temperance, which is one of the Fruit of the Spirit that lets us know that too much of anything, even a good thing, can be not so good for us.

So as you take in all of this data from all of these sources, the analysis of the information can lead to the loss of ability to move. You may have begun your journey to fulfillment and purpose with a clear starting point in mind; but, after consuming all of the various things from multiple sources, you become confused about where to start or which way is the right way for you, and guess what… you become stuck. You have all of this great insight on how things could be through all of the different avenues out there, and you stand there like you're at a fork in the road without a roadmap.

This is what we refer to as analysis paralysis. So, as your purpose midwife, I would encourage you to do your research and connect with people who give you hope on your journey, but don't go the over-consume and under-digest route. It is okay to connect to the resources and to take in information that helps you grow, but don't neglect to put those actions into play and keep moving forward on your journey.

For many of you, your purpose is full-term, and it is time to push! If you are tired of carrying around purpose and not fulfilling it, I would love to be your purpose midwife. I am passionate about healthy purpose birthing practices, safe delivery space, and the nurturing necessary once your purpose has been delivered.

All you need is one big push!

What are you ready to push forward?

What are you going to need to do in order to push your purpose into this world? What resources or degrees will be necessary? Now is the time to get clear on the steps that it will take in order for you to live a life of purpose.

_____

_____

_____

_____

_____

_____

Post-Pardon Me While
I Live on Purpose!

*"Now that I have birthed this new mindset,
I ask that you pardon me as I live the rest
of my life on purpose."*

-Brandi Ray

PARDON IS OFTEN USED when you are attempting to maneuver around people who are not moving in the direction you are headed in. Once you begin operating in this new mindset, I want to prepare you for the necessity to pardon yourself. Not everyone around you will shift when you shift; there will be situations and people that you may have to excuse yourself from to pursue purpose.

You have worked hard through the pages of this book identifying broke mindsets, pinpointing places of brokenness, and speaking life to your barrenness, but this is not your stopping point. There is still work to do. I want you to give yourself permission to follow your dreams, chase change, and pursue purpose.

WARNING: PURPOSE PURSUIT UNDERWAY!

About the Author

Brandi Ray is a wife, a mother, a court reporter by profession, but a tremendously passionate purpose pursuer and pusher by calling.

Although successful in her career pursuits, Brandi felt like there was so much more that she was created to birth into this world. So she began on her on-purpose journey that took many different twists and turns throughout the years. Still, one thing that never changed was that it was her way with words and her ability to believe that which was yet to be seen in herself and others, that was her truest self and her highest calling.

In this book, Brandi shares with you how life once made her feel less than her God-given best and the changes in her mind and her actions that allowed her to shift the trajectory of her life and access the abundance that was awaiting her on the other side of labor and delivery of her purpose.

Brandi has carried her purpose to term, birthed it, and now she is ready to share that purpose with the world so that she can be fruitful and multiply the gift that God placed in her while she was under attack, even in her mother's womb. Many in her small community have witnessed the gift that Brandi possesses and experienced the empowering of her words and her faith, and through this book, she would like to share that gift with you.

To contact Brandi to be your purpose midwife through purpose coaching or for more resources to assist you on your journey, please visit:

www.brandiray.online

If you have an event and you would like me to bring forth an impactful, motivational, and most importantly, transformational message, please book all speaking at www.brandiray.online or via email:

purposepursuerpreneur@gmail.com

Made in the USA
Middletown, DE
26 May 2022